You Are The Difference PRINCIPLES

The way a person feels does effect how they behave which in turn effects the results they achieve. *You Are The Difference* works because not only does it help people to think differently about the customer it also helps them to think differently about themselves and the service they give.

When the Skills and Techniques within the *You Are The Difference* Customer Service Coaching Programme are used on the shop floor everyone wins. The business wins because the level of service and customer conversion is increased resulting in happier customers and greater sales. The sales team wins because they are given a simple and effective way to help them interact with the customer making their role within the store more rewarding and effective. The customer wins because they receive a level of service second to none.

By applying the *You Are The Difference* principles within the role as a store manager or sales advisor a person will:

• Develop the skills, knowledge and confidence in how to welcome, engage and close the sale in a natural, non-pressurised way.

• Create a positive momentum within the store; impacting on the way the whole team thinks about customer service.

• Encourage the customer to re-visit the store by the high level of service provided.

The *You Are The Difference* Customer Service Coaching Programme is unique. It was developed on the shop floor through years of working with thousands of REAL customers. Each skill has been perfected to help both the retailer and the customer enjoy a perfect shop floor relationship...in short it DELIVERS!

Note for Librarians: A cataloguing record for this book is available from Library and Archives Canada at www.collectionscanada.ca/amicus/index-e.html

ISBN 1-4120-9413-5

Printed and bound by Thomson Litho Ltd, East Kilbride, Scotland

Printed in Victoria, BC, Canada. Printed on paper with minimum 30% recycled fibre. Trafford's print shop runs on "green energy" from solar, wind and other environmentally-friendly power sources.

Offices in Canada, USA, Ireland and UK

Book sales for North America and international:
Trafford Publishing, 6E–2333 Government St.,
Victoria, BC V8T 4P4 CANADA
phone 250 383 6864 (toll-free 1 888 232 4444)
fax 250 383 6804; email to orders@trafford.com

Book sales in Europe:
Trafford Publishing (UK) Limited, 9 Park End Street, 2nd Floor
Oxford, UK OX1 1HH UNITED KINGDOM
phone +44 (0)1865 722 113 (local rate 0845 230 9601)
facsimile +44 (0)1865 722 868; info.uk@trafford.com

Order online at:
trafford.com/06-1168

20   19   18   17   16   15   14   13   12

SOME OF THE COMPANIES THAT HAVE EXPERIENCED
You Are The Difference PROGRAMMES

Marks and Spencer

McArthurGlen Designer Outlet Shopping Centres

Aker Kvaener

Levis

The Body Shop

Wedgwood

Aberdeen Football Club

Whittington Hospital

Mothercare

Perthshire City Traders

First UK Bus

Cotton Traders

Thorntons

Adams Children's Wear

Selfridges

Carlton George Hotels

Lunn Polly

Mountain Warehouse

Moss Bros

Stead and Simpson

Jaeger

Cornwall Retail Trust

Hallmark

Iron Bed Company

Co-op

Staffa Health

Sharps Bedrooms

Jumper

Martin McColl

John Lewis

Brand - Fusion

Regatta

Calvin Klein

Although your customers won't love you if you give bad service, your competitors will.

WHAT PEOPLE HAVE SAID ABOUT
You Are The Difference

'I found the session, enjoyable, stimulating but above all simple. It was obvious that if the principles talked about were put into practice there must be benefits to not only companies "bottom lines" but people's morale. Alf Dunbar's passion and enthusiasm made it a pleasure for all who were present'

Michael Green
Chief Executive
British Council of Shopping Centres

'The **You Are The Difference** and **Living our Customer First** work that Alf led at Marks and Spencer was excellent. People came away very positive and ready to try out the practical methods that he gave them. The Marks and Spencer Outlet team found the **Living our Customer First** simple to understand and in using it felt more confident in selling to customers.'

Richard Wolff
Director- International and UK outlets
Marks and Spencer PLC

'This man is a genius!
I have witnessed the affect that Alf has on staff of all ages, the level of motivation they leave with after his training is outstanding and his simple techniques lead directly to improved sales.
If every retailer implemented the simple techniques detailed in this book then bad service would finally become a thing of the past.'

John O'Shea
SCEPTRE Awards Shopping Centre Manager of the year 2006
(Medium Sized Centres)
Freeport Braintree Outlet Shopping Village

'Alf has been working in partnership with Thorntons to deliver the *You are the Difference* Programme embedding the techniques into a way of working within our stores. Our Store Managers left the course excited and feeling positive. The techniques are so simple to understand it was easy for them to coach their store teams and more importantly it really worked and improved their sales and transactional value! This partnership has developed further with Alf helping to provide innovative solutions to improve sales performance through other coaching programmes.'

Joanne Attenborough
Head of HR
Thorntons plc

'Alf Dunbar is an inspirational presenter. He kept our audience of 50 plus enthralled for the afternoon with his positive messages and dynamism. His simple person centered approach to making the best of life and work for the individual and customer has improved our environment for patients and staff. The spiral of positivity has been a key addition to the office and nobody wants to be the NEG. Thanks for letting us see that we are in control and can make a difference'

Valerie Beattie
General Practice Manager
Staffa Health Derbyshire

'*You Are The Difference* has made a real impact throughout our business. All of our customers, both internal and external, are enjoying higher levels of service as a result of the customer service programme. A significant number of our team have commented on how *You Are The Difference* has changed their attitude to life outside of the working environment as well as in it. This has been an unexpected, but most welcome benefit'

Nick Hamblin
Retail Director
Cotton Traders

'Alf Dunbar entered my world approx 6 years ago and completely blew me away with an exciting, very powerful and new concept of Customer Service training.

I strongly recommend anyone who is connected in any way with the service industry to give it a try – you too will become one of the converted.'

Cheryl Sadler
Centre Manager
Lakeside Village Outlet Shopping Centre

'Through the **You Are The Difference** programme Alf has made the delivery of outstanding customer service and path to extra sales achievable for everyone.

His simple techniques are convincing, easy to follow and highly motivational. I can safely say that this is the most compelling programme I have come across in twenty years in retail.

I have found Alf's programmes to be inspirational not only professionally but also in my private life.'

Bill Godwin
Retail Operations Manager REALM Limited
Retail Property and Asset Management

'I first met Alf Dunbar at a Chamber of Commerce business breakfast in February this year and, for 8 am in the morning, was impressed by the way which he captivated and engaged an audience of some 250 people which is why I was keen for him to come and give his take on customer service to managers. As someone who has many years' experience in the retail trade, he is an ideal person to be able to coach and train on how to offer outstanding customer service, something we in John Lewis Aberdeen are striving for every time we acknowledge a customer.'

Robert Garnish
Operations and Selling Support Manager
John Lewis

'With unique insight, Alf has put together an educational and motivational training package that can be delivered through all levels of the business.

From the Saturday sales assistant to the most commercial of managers *You Are The Difference* has made an 'incredible difference' to the dynamics and performance of the teams in this business.

The very nature of this simple, powerful and yet practical program gave confidence and self empowerment to all.

By embracing and delivering the skills and effective techniques from the programme, sales have risen and customer service standards have improved. What more can I say? It's the best shop floor coaching programme to come along in years.'

Jane McLeoud
Centre Manager
Atlantic Village Outlet Shopping and Attractions

'I first met Alf at the BCSC Centre Managers conference and was impressed by the way he captivated and engaged with the audience. I felt it would be great for Alf to come and present The *You Are the Difference* course to all the team at St James Shopping and Multrees Walk. The session he ran was interactive, educational and practical. The simple but effective messages have provided all staff with the skills and confidence to deliver outstanding customer service.'

Rochelle Weir
General Manager
St James Shopping and Multrees Walk

'*You Are The Difference* has been taken on wholeheartedly within Chapelle and the positive effects on our team focus and the quality of customer service in our stores were immediately apparent. Certainly a refreshing approach to maximising sales in our stores.'

Paul Mortimer
Managing Director
Chapelle Jewellery

'Alf Dunbar proved that the techniques delivered in his successful *You Are The Difference* programme can be adapted to suit any business environment. When Alf ran an adaptation of his course to our Call Centre and Operations staff, he delivered the same powerful message that he uses in his Retail Coaching Sessions about how the individual can obtain empowerment by their own thought processes and actions. The methodology Alf uses is simplistic, yet so powerful, that even the most negative person can be inspired. The results have been amazing.The *You Are The Difference* coaching session has made a difference!'

Gail Jones
Head of Operations
Cotton Traders

'Alf was introduced to us by one of our trading partners Thorntons PLC. His unique style of delivery helps people to remember the principles within *You Are The Difference* which cannot fail to deliver more sales to any customer facing business. Our business strives to attain a culture of going the extra mile for our customers and this has been significantly aided by the *You Are The Difference* customer service programme. I would thoroughly recommend *You Are The Difference* to anyone that deals with customers, I think that is most of us!'

Stanley Morrice
Managing Director
McLeish Brothers Ltd

'A lot of companies talk about great customer service but the challenge is to ensure this happens day in day out. To achieve this you need to train, train and retrain staff using simple methods. This is what attracted us to *You are the Difference*. Whenever our staff go through this training they all agree that it's simple and achievable'.

David Sands
Managing Director
David Sands Ltd

'Having worked in Retail for over 30 years and been totally committed to the Customer, the challenge still remains for every person in our/any company to have that shared commitment. Since working with Alf and his team I have been totally amazed by the response individuals have made in taking ownership in ensuring the customer leaves the store with the same level of service they themselves would like to experience — 'people do buy people first'. *You Are The Difference* has lead to a positive sales increase within our business and now we now look forward to rolling the programme out as part of our overall training/coaching development.'

Dominic Prendergast
Retail Director Thorntons

'I have worked with Alf Dunbar for approximately 6 years since we launched *"You Are The Difference"* to our International Franchise customers.
Many of our customers comment on the simple yet effective messages that the programme conveys and it's simplicity is one of the strongest selling points - it works in any language. We have now rolled this out across 25 countries and for many of them it continues to be an integral part of their store induction process.'

Carole Ohl
International HR and Learning Manager
Marks and Spencer
International Franchise Group

'It was the best learning experience I have ever had. I felt a confidence inside that makes me excited about trying out the new skills as soon as I can.
Everything I have been taught will benefit not only myself but the customer and the company.'

Amanda Pool
Sales Supervisor
Reebok

CONTENTS

Acknowledgements   13

Introduction   19

How it all began   21

Choices   25

You Are The Difference   31

1.   The Elephant and the Stick   31
2.   People Buy People First   35
3.   Love or Loathe   37
4.   Priorities   39
5.   Lifetime Value of a Customer   41
6.   The Spiral of Positivity   45
5.   Greeting the Customer   55
6.   A Relaxed Approach   61
7.   Perfect Partners   65
8.   Closing the Sale   67
9.   Product in the Hand   69
10. The Fitting Room   73
11. The Fab Five: At the Till   75
12. The Magnificent Seven: Recap   77
13. Catch a Butterfly   79
14. Reach for Your Best   81

The Role of the Manager in *You Are The Difference*   83
Barriers   84
Circle of Control   85
Five Stages of Coaching   88
B-Alert   89

Take Action   92

The Personal Goal   95

*Want to Know More About **You Are The Difference**?*   97

Customer service is an attitude; not a department.

www.youarethedifference.co.uk

ACKNOWLEDGMENTS

THANK YOU

To my wonderful children Lisa and Christian and to my stepson Jacob who remind me how lucky I am to be a father.

To my family for their never ending support.

To my friends David and Ann Lawtie, Adrian Hughes and Steven Boyle who are always there for me.

To the Odense team who helped me start it all and worked so hard, Therese Gibney, Lone Markuslund, Vibe Johansson, Rikke Nielsen, Helle Jorgensen and Laila Rietbergen.

To Vince and Tanya Gunn, Teresa Nicholls, Andrea Bennett, Lizzie Robinson and Hilary Black for believing in the programme and in me.

To James Cook and the team at Trafford Publishing for their guidance, help and advice.

To Rima and Zaine Sawaya for their help and original ideas, to Les Clark, Joyce Scott, Roddy Jameison, Craig Johnston and Trevor Runcie for their patience and talent.

To my clients and colleagues who always motivate me with their enthusiasm.

Customers are not an interruption of our work; they are the purpose of it.

This book is dedicated to all those people everywhere who spend their working day in the service of others.

If good customer service was easy, everyone would be doing it!

MY CONTRACT

I...

Commit myself to finding the time I need to read this book. I am ready to practice the skills and techniques set out within the *You Are The Difference* Programme and I will do all I can to reach for my best.

I agree to focus on giving the best customer service I can.

Signature......................................

Date..

There is a difference between interest and commitment. When you're interested in doing something, you do it only when it's convenient.
When you're committed to something you accept no excuses, only results.

Ken Blanchard

If we don't take care of our customers; someone else will.

INTRODUCTION

In every country around the world every single day millions of people are working in the retail industry.

People choose to work within retail for many different reasons; for some it's a weekend or casual job while for others it can be a full time career that can span a lifetime.

Having worked as a performance coach with the *You Are The Difference* customer service programme for the past 10 years throughout the UK, Europe and the Middle East, I've become increasingly aware that there is a real need for an easy to understand, effective book and DVD that together satisfy two requirements.Firstly, to help store managers and sales advisors to get the most from their daily interaction, both as a team and with the customer on the shop floor: and secondly to answer a question I am asked repeatedly, i.e. "How can we coach our sales teams the *You Are The Difference* programme AND keep it alive long-term so it becomes part of our shop floor culture?"

I believe the *Just Looking Thanks!* book and DVD coaching package provides the answer.

Here is a typical situation a new person starting out in retail can find her or himself in; perhaps some people will recognise this scenario.

First day in the job and you feel a little nervous. You make your way onto the shop floor; there are strangers every-where, the customers!

You then think to yourself, "What do I do with all these customers? What do I say to them? How should I act with them?"

You then start to draw on your own experiences as a customer.

So you say to the first customer, "Can I help you?" or "Are you all right there?" or "Need any help?"

Do you like it when this happens when you are shopping as a customer? No! Does it work? No! Will you say this on your first day? Yes! And will it work? NO! Result: a bad initial experience on your very first day by having customers continually saying to you,"Just looking thanks!" and already a growing lack of confidence working on the shop floor.

That experience seems to be what many new people working in retail have had on their first day in the job! It's almost become like a continuous circle and it needs to be broken!

When the skills and techniques within this book are used on the shop floor everyone wins. The business wins because the level of service and customer conversion is increased resulting in happier customers and greater sales. The manager wins because they are able to lead, motivate and coach the team, keeping the *You Are The Difference* programme alive and helping it to become part of the service culture in their store. The salesperson wins because they are given a simple and effective way to help them interact more easily with the customer making their role on the shop floor more rewarding and effective. The customer wins because they receive a level of service second to none.

We are what we repeatedly do.
Excellence then is not an act, but a habit.

Aristotle

HOW IT ALL BEGAN

In late 1991, I moved from Aberdeen (Scotland) to Odense in Denmark. My Danish girlfriend Bodil was pregnant at that time and wanted to be nearer her family. I didn't speak Danish and was concerned about my employment prospects so I began looking into starting my own business. I had worked in retail for the previous seven years and had always enjoyed working with customers so opening a store seemed the obvious choice.

I had friends that owned a skin/hair care retail franchise in Aberdeen and as they were always positive about the business I decided to look at the possibilities of opening a similar franchise in Denmark.

After a few months of searching we secured a good location in the city of Odense, Denmark's third largest city. It was a large, old store with lots of potential but as with most shop fits, especially when it comes to old premises, there are usually hidden costs. This store was to prove no exception. The total opening costs quickly rose much higher than the original budget which meant more funding was required, resulting in an extra large bank overdraft. This was not how I had seen the business starting out. We then set about doing all we could to get the turnover up to a level that would help us to reduce the debt as fast as possible.

We seemed to struggle along for the first few years always having to work very long hours for what appeared to be little or no return.

Lisa, our daughter was born just before the store opened and for the first six months of her life she came with us every day. During those 6 months I became quite an expert at serving customers with one hand while holding Lisa with the other. This seemed to take the customers attention away from the fact that I couldn't speak the language properly. They would be busy looking at Lisa while I tried to work out how to pronounce the product in Danish!

It seemed nothing we did made any real impact on our growing debt. Any extra profit we did make at Christmas (December accounted for over 30% of our annual turnover) seemed to instantly disappear on bank charges and extra costs.

In our third year of trading we were then approached by the Head Franchisee responsible for the running of Danish operations about opening a second store in the nearby town of Svendborg.

As Odense and Svendborg carried the main population of Fyn (the island we lived on) we felt having the two stores would give us exclusivity and be a good move.

The Head Franchisee suggested that if we went ahead they would give us favourable terms on a loan to finance the shop fit and help with the first six months stock.

On paper this all looked like a good idea and one that could secure the business for the future.

Once finished, the new Svendborg store, which was on two floors, looked amazing.

In the first few months it did well. However it never took off the way we had planned. The local competition in Svendborg was very tough and the customers were proving to be very loyal to our main competitor, which had traded in the town for a generation.

The team in Svendborg were very committed and everyone put in a huge effort but within a couple of years we had to admit defeat. The store was never going to make the money we expected.

Around this time our Head Franchisee made it clear to us that unless we were able to repay the monies we owed to them (which by this time was considerable) we would run the risk of losing both shops.

We continued to do everything we could to try to keep the business afloat but nothing we did seemed to make enough of a difference. We cut every single cost we could but the turnover was still far too low. We tried to sell the Svendborg store as a going concern but there was no interest so we decided as a last gasp effort to try and sell the leasehold.

Bodil then informed me that she had seen an advert for a new optical company based in Sweden that was looking to expand into Denmark. She said she would call and inquire if they would be interested in a store in Svendborg. At first I didn't give the idea much of a chance, "Why would a large Swedish company be interested in our store in Svendborg?" At best I felt it was a long shot.

After a few days I had forgotten all about the idea of approaching the Swedish company when out of the blue came a call; they were sending some people from their head office to have a look at the store!

Within a month they had been to the store and made us an offer to buy out the lease! The money we received took some of the pressure off and kept the Odense store afloat.

Looking back, that experience changed my perception about things; here I was thinking, "We're finished, we're going to lose it all," when what I really needed was a positive outlook and to be open to new ideas.

From then on, I felt things were beginning to change.

In this competitive age customers do not depend on us, we depend on them.

CHOICES

A month after the store in Svendborg was sold we decided to take some time off and stay with some friends in Copenhagen over the weekend. Their flat was so small it resulted in us having to sleep on the lounge floor! That decision was to prove to be a major factor in what happened next. The morning after our arrival I awoke early, and while trying to find something to read while everyone else was still asleep, I found a book lying on the floor next to me. It must have fallen from the bookshelf during the night. It got my attention as the title was in English while all the other books I could see were in Danish. The title of the book was *CHOICES*. It was a small book that looked a bit old and tattered but it had an interesting title so I started reading the first page:

"We DO live out the lives that our programmes create for us.
Any of us, when we choose can give ourselves new programmes!
What an incredible opportunity that fact gives you. The choices you make NEXT are up to you. That is what this book is all about."
-Shad Hemstitcher

Within 3 days I had read the book. Twice! I just could not put it down.
Reading that book helped me to understand that I was 'choosing' many of the results in my business up to that point. There was nothing to be gained in blaming circumstances or other people for the state it was in, which was something I had been doing up till then.

I was the one that needed to make some new choices and turn things around.
What if I CHOSE to change the way I ran the Odense store and how I treated our customers. What if I CHOSE to interact with customers in a totally different way and CHOSE to give them a new experience in service? What if I made the CHOICE to sell much more, 50% more for example?

I decided to raise the matter with the management of the Head Franchise in Denmark. I met with them and explained the new ideas in terms of customer service and management.

I argued that I could turn the business around and pay back all the money I owed.

All I asked was that they trusted me for a little while and were patient.

To their credit and my surprise the franchise management agreed. I immediately set out to plan the new way forward.

The customer service skills and techniques you will read as you progress through this book were all developed working on the Odense shop floor. None of the techniques came from a book or old training programme; everything was developed through thousands of contacts with real customers.

In the beginning when I started working on the new techniques it was all a bit trial and error but that was to my advantage as it showed me what DIDN'T work. Over time and constant interaction with customers, the techniques started to take real shape.

With everyone in the team agreeing to get behind the new ideas the turnover began to slowly climb and there was also a huge shift in attitude amongst the staff. Everyone had become much more positive and there was a real buzz beginning to grow in the store.

I used many different ways to keep the team focused and on track but the best result by far came from coaching the staff individually on the shop floor, and by leading from the front by serving customers myself.

After around 12 months of working with the techniques, the store results had increased by an amazing 42% compared with Denmark's overall annual growth rate of 12%. This attracted the attention of the franchise HQ. A representative from the company visited Denmark and came to Odense to have a look at what we were up to. She wanted to know why our figures were so good.

I explained to her how we had turned things around and just how reliable these techniques were.

I asked to be allowed to try the new techniques back in Britain.

I was eager to prove that they could work anywhere. If I could show just how successful I could be with the techniques in a store I had never worked in before, people would have to take notice. I truly believed I had developed a programme that could be used in any store anywhere in the world.

The representative could immediately feel the buzz in the store and became very positive about the idea and said she would do all they could to help me get the HQ's attention.

Shortly after that visit I won the 'Denmark Manager of the Year' award and part of the prize was a trip to the UK to receive my trophy.

As I had a free day in London, I seized the opportunity to visit some of their top stores with the aim of observing their sales techniques and customer service and to try to capture top management's attention with my proposal to address weaknesses, if any! I visited three stores on one street alone which had a larger turnover than all the fifteen stores in Denmark combined! This was a different world.

In truth, I was a little concerned about my plan at the time. After all, here I was setting out to go mystery shopping in their stores, perhaps to discover things that were not as they should be, when they had actually been generous enough to have paid for my trip to London. However, I felt this was a one-off opportunity and I had to make my mark.

I went to eight stores and after each visit I wrote a short report. Some of it didn't make good reading but I quickly became aware of the huge opportunities there were in the UK; I was starting to get excited!

When I presented the report to the Head of UK Management I was surprised that he didn't send me back on the next flight to Denmark. Instead he immediately asked his two right-hand people to listen to my report. I could see they were not happy with what they were hearing but to their credit they sat quietly and took it all in.

After a few days of lengthy discussion it was organised for me to work in a London store for a full day to try and produce some kind of result that would back up my claims about the techniques I had developed.

I clearly remember I didn't sleep much the night before the day I was to work in the trial store. I knew that this would be my one and only chance to back up my claims about the techniques. I had to get it right.

As I walked to the store early that day I remember imagining there was a person from my team in Denmark on each street corner encouraging me and saying I could do it.

Visualising their encouragement seemed to help me focus and give me the confidence that I could do it.

After I arrived at the store, which was in a busy side street, I explained to the staff why I was there and what we were going to do that day. As they all stood there looking at each other in silence the shop manager announced that they would all be proud to help make it happen. At that point I knew we had a chance.

That day was one I will never forget. It all went to plan. As soon as I started using the techniques they worked and the sales that followed were fantastic.

By the time the store closed we had sold over 25% more than the normal turnover for that day!

The feeling I had at the end of that long day was one of elation: everything I had believed in had worked. The fact it worked as well in the UK as it did in Denmark convinced me that the techniques could overcome any cultural barrier and they could work anywhere.

After the success in the trial store it was agreed that I would work in a major store in London for a period of three months. The store had not been achieving its true potential and it was felt that if my new methods could work anywhere then turning this store around would be the proof the business needed to roll out the new techniques across the rest of the chain.

The next three months were perhaps the most difficult and challenging time I have ever faced. The store was in a prime position in the centre of London and had a huge flow of customers. At busy periods during the day it felt like it was the Christmas rush back in my store in Denmark!

My first challenge was the number of staff in this store. There were over thirty! I only had four in my store!

This meant lots of individual and group coaching covering many different shift patterns resulting in very long hours but I knew if I didn't get all the staff behind me we would fail. The sheer volume of customers meant anything I did as an individual would be minute in comparison to what we could achieve if I got everyone working as a team and using the new techniques. Fortunately for me there were some brilliant people working in that store and very soon everyone rallied around and we started to go forward.

At the end of the three-month trial the store had increased its turnover by some £30,000 and was performing brilliantly! I owe much gratitude to those people who worked so hard with me on that shop floor. They did a great job.

Following the three-month trial I spent the next year as a Training Consultant for the company, travelling around the country coaching more store teams.

For that purpose I had to put together a short coaching session so the new skills and techniques could be taught to managers and staff in a professional way. As I had no previous experience in coaching at that time I thought the best way to do it was to design a coaching session that I would enjoy if I were the trainee.

I had been to many different types of training sessions over the years so I knew exactly what I didn't want! I was determined to make it motivational, educational and fun; above all else people would have a good time and remember it; after all I came to the conclusion that if people are laughing they must be listening.

On the train journey to the company's headquarters where I would start putting together the session I came up with the title *You Are The Difference*. I was reading a newspaper article about how a high street bank wanted to be very different and the word 'different' stood out. The coaching session was about the customer and the difference the people working in the store could make through giving great service so *You Are The Difference* sounded and felt right.

After that success I set up my own company with one of the company's top managers: Energize Learning Partnership. Very quickly we managed to get the attention of some of the top retailers in the country and work with them. Our partnership lasted successfully for four years then we parted ways as we developed other interests.

YOU ARE THE DIFFERENCE

The *You Are The Difference* Customer Service Coaching Programme is unique. It was developed on the shop floor through years of working with thousands of REAL customers. Each skill has been perfected to help both the retailer and the customer enjoy a perfect shop floor relationship...in short it DELIVERS!

Have you ever been to the zoo and seen the elephants? Have you ever noticed that they are only tied to a small stick in the ground with a thin rope? Why doesn't the elephant just pull on the rope and run away? The reason it doesn't is because when it was a baby it had one of its legs tied with a chain to a large tree. The baby elephant would then pull on the chain for days but would never manage to break free. In the end, it gave up and stood still.

Later in life despite being a fully-grown elephant, if there is even a thin rope tied around its leg and then attached to a small stick in the ground it will just stand still.

Why? Because the elephant lets *previous behaviour affect it later in life*.

Why is this relevant to you?
Don't let anything you have done in the past stop you from using the skills and techniques in this book. You CAN master them all - it's a bit like crossing an invisible line. Instead of thinking, "Will I?" or "Won't I?" just step over the line. It's always much easier than you thought and once you have taken the initial step you will find you can then take another, then another, and another...

Now have a look at the second elephant below. It's pulled on the rope and ran away!

It's become motivated; it's become positive enough to make it happen.

Very often before I run sessions people come up to me and ask, "Are you here to get us all motivated? To make us feel all positive?"

It's interesting that being positive can't make you do anything. Let's look at that statement again.

"BEING POSITIVE CAN'T MAKE YOU DO ANYTHING!"

Let's face it, I could get really positive but I couldn't save your life by giving you heart surgery! I could get really positive but I could never beat a champion boxer in the ring!

No, being positive can't make you do anything but it will help you to do EVERYTHING better than NEGATIVE thinking will. Would you agree with that statement?

As you read through this book you will start to make decisions about its contents and some of these decisions will be emotional ones - a bit like those we make on New Year's Eve and break the very next day! In order for a decision to become a commitment it needs to be reaffirmed over and over again. That commitment can then lead to behaviour change.

New behaviour that can help you to step over that line - to become the winner you know you can be, the winner you know you DESERVE to be!

Good customer service is the cheapest and most effective form of advertising.

PEOPLE BUY PEOPLE FIRST
THE PRODUCT SECOND

Imagine you are walking down a main shopping street or that you are in a shopping centre.
You suddenly remember there is a product you need.
You see a store close by and you think to yourself, "I'll try in there." You find the product you need and you take it to the till. There you experience BAD service. The sales person doesn't look up at you; they take the product, ring up the price, take your money, return your change, then shout "NEXT" to the customer behind you.

Around a month later you are in that same street or shopping centre and you remember you need that same product again. You see the store where you bought it last time but you notice another shop that may stock the product a little further away. This time you decide to try in this other store.
In this store you find the same product at the same price. You take it to the till and this time you receive GREAT service! The sales person looks up and greets you. She/he comments on how good the product you bought is, places your change in your hand, smiles and says thank you and goodbye.

The next time you are shopping in that same street or shopping centre and you need that product again, which store would YOU choose?
The FIRST or the SECOND?

The Second. Why?
People buy people first the product second – **FACT!**
Try to think about the last time you received good customer service?
If you can remember it you will probably remember something about the PERSON.
It sticks out in the mind because it's NOT the norm.

Treat every customer as if they sign your pay cheque-because they do.

THINGS WE LOVE OR LOATHE TO EXPERIENCE IN SERVICE

Can you see the difference between good and bad service when you shop?

I'm sure you can, after all you are also a customer. Think how many stores you have visited during your lifetime. Based on your experience as a customer try to complete the lists below choosing in the LOVE column 5 things you love to experience in service and in the other, 5 things you LOATHE. This isn't about the colour of the store carpet or the style of the lighting but the quality of the service the staff give you when you shop.

LOVE ♥   LOATHE !@^*^@*

✓   X

✓   X

✓   X

✓   X

✓   X

Take a close look at the two lists you have now completed above. Imagine these are two different stores selling similar products. Which store would you always choose to go back to?

What type of service do you usually experience when you shop; the LOVE or the LOATHE?

Now look again at the Love column! How many of those listed could people working in a store easily CHOOSE to do? Almost all of them!

But why is it when we shop we experience so many of those in the Loathe column?

I believe it's because in many stores the sales team's focus is elsewhere.

What would happen if a store chose to give their customers a level of service similar to that of the Love column? Would you agree those customers would come back again and again?

All this sounds simple and straightforward but it's my experience and probably yours that none of this can begin to start happening unless the people who manage the store and work on the shop floor commit to making the right choices around customer service.

1. To deliver a 'Love' service requires making a CHOICE to do so.

2. Customers will always choose to return to the store that gives the 'Love' service.

3. The Manager of the store will always influence where the shop floor focus will be.

If you would like to see some of the TOP Loves and Loathes people have listed from previous *You Are The Difference* sessions please turn to page 93.

PRIORITIES

When we look at the shop floor there are 4 main priorities. In no particular order they are; Visual Merchandising (VM), the Staff, the Customer, and Tasks (e.g. paperwork, cleaning, filling-up etc.). If we had to put these four in some kind of order of 1 to 4 with 1 being the most important, where would you place them?

I'm going to guess that you put the Customer as number 1, the Staff number 2, followed by Tasks then Visual Merchandising - you may have put VM as number 3 then Tasks as 4 but it's more likely that you will put the Customer first. During the coaching sessions I run, almost everyone agrees the Customer is number 1. Occasionally a person from the group will shout out that the team is Number 1! This usually causes a revolt in the room; "YES!" Everyone will then shout out, "The Staff are number 1". I then ask, "What if we have the best staff in the world and no customers?" The room then falls silent and everyone then agrees that the CUSTOMER must be the number 1.

At every session I have run, people in the end agree that the customer must be the number 1, BUT do we always live it? When we are working on the shop floor do we put the customer before the tasks?

Imagine you have a day off and you decide to go on a shopping trip with a friend. You reach the shopping/city centre and start window shopping when suddenly you see a store you have visited recently that had a product on sale you really liked.

"Come on," you say to your friend, "Let me show you what I saw the other day, it really looked great!" However, as you enter the store you notice the layout is a little different from the last time you visited. So with a slightly confused look you start looking around for the product that you wanted to show to your friend. Meanwhile over in the corner two of the staff are working together tidying the stock with their backs to you. One is saying to the other, "Not that busy is it?" while the other replies, "I know! Not seen many customers at all today!" Meanwhile you are still looking around confused and a bit lost.

Just freeze that frame for a second: where is the customer in terms of care and attention on our scale of 1 to 4 at that point? Yes, number 4 and where is tasks? Number 1! What would happen if a shop lived the customer as number 4 and tasks as number 1? The business would suffer.

But customers don't go up to staff and say, "You don't live us first."

That's not how they tell us is it?

So how do they tell us? Usually by walking out!

The next time you are working on the shop floor ask yourself this question: Where is my attention? Because wherever it is at that point, THAT is your number 1 priority. If you imagine a see-saw and the customer is at one end and tasks are at the other, it's a case of getting the balance right. Of course the tasks have to be done but the CUSTOMER must always come FIRST.

WHAT IS THE LIFETIME VALUE OF A CUSTOMER?

This poses an interesting question: just how much is a customer actually worth?

Every day on every shop floor sales people spend a huge amount of time and effort helping and advising customers - but what happens to all that time and effort long-term? Where does it all go?

Here is a simple exercise that gives an approximate amount each customer could be worth financially. The figures below are only an approximation; try putting your own company's figures into the scheme on the next page and see just how much your customers are potentially really worth!

Average shopping lifetime of a customer   approx 40 years

Average visits in a year   approx 12 (One per month min)

Average spend per visit   approx £30

40 years multiplied by 12 visits per year   480 visits

480 multiplied by £30   £14400

TOTAL   **£14400**

So there it is. If you have a regular customer that spends £30 on average once a month and they shop with you over a lifetime that covers 40 years, they are worth over £14000!! You can instantly see all your time and effort IS worth it! And remember that's only if they spend £30. What if it's much more than that and they shop 2 to 3 times a month? The figure then keeps going up and up!

CUSTOMER LIFETIME VALUE: EXAMPLE

Try the exercise with your own stores figures:

Average shopping lifetime of an average customer

Approx years   = (   )

Average visits to the store in a month

Approx (   ) x 12 = Total visits in 12 months = (   )

Average spend per visit £   = (   )

Total amount of years multiplied by total amount of visits in 12 months = Lifetime visits

Total years (   ) x Total visits (   )   = (   )

Total amount of lifetime visits multiplied by average spend

Total visits (   ) x Average spend (   )

TOTAL   £(   )

There you have it... the potential lifetime value of just ONE of your customers!

THE QUIET COMPLAINER
And
THE CUSTOMER CHAMPION

Do you ever wonder what happens when a store gives bad customer service? Well, it's as if that store gives a gift to its competition. It's a bit like the store has said "There you are, here is £14000 (using the previous lifetime value), we don't really want it, it's all yours.
Moreover, you create...

THE QUIET COMPLAINER

The quiet complainer tends not to tell the store they are unhappy with the level of service, but they usually tell others – making word of mouth work against the store.

However, if you do give a customer good service you create...
THE CUSTOMER CHAMPION

• The champion is very valuable to your business.

• The champion will shop regularly with you!

• The champion will tell other people how good the service is in your store and can be your best form of advertising!

• The champion spends on average **£14000** over their lifetime with you! (Using our example)

• When you look at the above it's clear that your time and effort with a customer IS worth it!

The spiral of positivity is the FOUNDATION of *You Are The Difference*.

The spiral affects all aspects of your life: in the home, the workplace, everywhere.
In fact it travels with us wherever we go!

RAINING
NO MILK
TRAFFIC
ILLNESS
STOCK MOVES
CUSTOMERS

CRASH!

Imagine ...
It's early one Monday morning; you are tucked up fast asleep when suddenly your alarm goes off. "Oh no," you think, then say to yourself, "It's ok, it's Friday." You feel a little better but then slowly, it dawns on you, it's Monday and you just had the weekend!
You get up and it's freezing. You go over to the window and open the curtains and you see it's raining. You make your way to the wardrobe to find what you will wear to work that day but it's not ironed.

You get yourself dressed and then make your way into the kitchen where you open the fridge and there is no milk! So there you are, eating your dry cornflakes and drinking your black cup of tea or coffee.

You then do what many people do in the morning, you switch on the radio or the TV or you pick up the paper and it's all BAD NEWS!

You leave for work; if you drive you get in the car and think, "please start" - it does but only on the 3rd attempt. You get to the junction and someone cuts right in front of you causing you to slam on the brakes and you think to yourself, "DRIVERS!!"

Or, you perhaps take the bus? You wait at the stop for what seems ages then two buses arrive together! Both are so full you have to stand the whole journey. Perhaps you walk to work? Someone has been out earlier walking their dog and you manage to step right in what it has left behind! It smells terrible!!

You finally make it into work where just before you go in you meet colleagues and you say, "Good Morning," to which they reply, "IS IT? Have you seen the weather? It's pouring. It will be dead today. Remember the last time it rained? DEAD!!"

You continue your way into the store and notice the rest of the team standing together shaking their heads and muttering, "It's going to be dead! Really DEAD!" Everyone is now on his or her way down the spiral.

You have been on the shop floor for only a short time when a team member runs up and says, "Have you seen who has called in sick AGAIN? Unbelievable! I'm going to tell everyone." Further down the spiral everyone falls.

A few hours pass when another person you work with comes past and comments, "Have you seen all the stock we have to move from one side of the store to the other? It was over there a few weeks ago and now they want us to put it back here!"

It's now mid-way through the afternoon and someone else comments, "What do they do with all this paper work? Look at all the stuff I am being asked to do! How can I serve customers when I am being asked to do all this?" Further down everyone slides.

It's now 5 minutes until the shop closes and all you want to do is to go home, take off your shoes, sit down and relax when in they come:

More customers!!

A team member cries out, "OH NO!"

The whole team then **CRASH!!**

This is a typical picture of what can happen in a store during the course of a day. Although in my experience, sometimes the sales team can be at the bottom of the spiral by mid morning!

It doesn't always have to be like that.

Imagine now that you have a day off and that you are at home enjoying a well earned break. You settle down to read a book or watch television. You are starting to relax when you suddenly hear this loud sound from outside: BEEB... BEEB...BEEB...You get up and look outside and there, you see this huge rubbish lorry reversing up to your front door.

Then you see its back trailer starting to tilt back. It's about to tip out all that rubbish, right there on YOUR front door step.

You have 2 options:

1. You can shrug your shoulders and go back to read your book or continue watching TV and put up with the rubbish and the smell, or:

2. You can go outside and shout, "**STOP!**

You're not dumping that rubbish here!"

Which of these 2 options would you choose? I hope that it would be the second option. Let's be honest, you would never let all that rubbish be dumped on your doorstep. But then why is it that we would allow people we know and work with to dump rubbish (another word for negativity) into our head, into the most valuable thing we have - OUR BRAIN! The thing that got us everything we have and everything we are going to have

When I go through this during a coaching session, some people comment to me:

"You just can't help but go down the spiral when those things happen - that's life!"

My response is always the same: "You are in control of your attitude."

That is really what the SPIRAL is all about - your attitude.

It's something that **you** and you alone control.

Imagine you are walking down a street and it's pouring rain; you are thinking to yourself:

"I really hate the rain!" when you notice a person walking towards you and as they pass you they comment, "Great weather eh! My grass will be looking great now!" It's all about how we perceive an event. Events don't carry a feeling, we give them one.

BE CAREFUL WHAT YOU FOCUS ON

Have you ever had someone say to you, "I'm going to buy this type of car in this colour," then all you see are those cars everywhere? Or someone tells you they are having a baby - then all you see are babies everywhere!

Where did they all come from?

The truth is they were always there; it's just when we think about something a lot it tends to turn up.

If we hadn't been thinking about that type of car or the baby they would of course still be there; we just wouldn't notice them as much.

So what's the point in all of this?

When we get up in the morning we tend to throw ourselves into our day, spending so much of the first hour getting ourselves ready and out the front door without really thinking about what we want out of that day. The first hour of every day is very important and can act a bit like a ship's rudder; if it's pointing in the wrong direction then we can set off on the wrong course and at times crash. We don't take those precious few moments to think about what we want to do with our day. In a sense we are not really awake. We go to work, meet a negative person, a NEG as I call them and allow them to pour rubbish (negativity) into our heads, pulling us down and down the spiral.

But what has all this got to do with customer service you might ask?

Well, **EVERYTHING!**

Have you ever been in a store where there is a negative customer service atmosphere on the shop floor? How does this make you feel as a customer?

Compare this to how you feel when you experience a positive customer service atmosphere? Would you agree you would be more likely to spend more time in that store and perhaps return there the next time you went shopping?

Sales teams that work hard to stay at the top of the spiral will always have a more enjoyable, positive day on the shop floor and there will always be much better atmosphere which the customer WILL notice.

FEEL-BEHAVIOUR-RESULT

Imagine that you are now employed as a sales representative for a company. You travel into the city and start knocking on doors. After a few hours of negative responses a company invites you in. The company is very interested in what you have to sell and you soon realise this could be a record sale for your business. Your new-found customer informs you that everything looks fine and that they will call you the next day to confirm everything.

On a scale of 1-10 with 1 being low and 10 being high how do you feel?
10 of course!!
Later that day you are supposed to give a short presentation to around 20 people. How do you feel the presentation will go?
I'm sure you will agree it will go very well.
The next day the company calls you about the order and informs you that they have decided to give the order to another supplier.
How do you feel on a scale of 1-10?
Probably 1 or 2!
Again you have to give that same presentation to another group of 20 people. How do you think this presentation will go this time?
Perhaps not so well. The fact is, how we FEEL does affect how we BEHAVE which will affect how well we perform and therefore the RESULTS we get.
If we arrive on the shop floor feeling low, let's say around a 2 or 3, then it's almost certain that our results at the end of the day will reflect this.
When I talk about the Feel-Behaviour-Result example during a coaching session I always ask the people in the audience if they feel I could run the session (which requires me to be very motivated and positive) if I was feeling a 3 or a 4 that day. The answer is always the same - the audience always agree it would be impossible for me to motivate them or hold their interest for 2 hours if I was as low as that, but some days I don't feel a 9 or a 10, I may wake up and feel

like a 3 or a 4. I think everyone can be like that on the odd day. How I deal with it is like this; I stop myself for a moment and focus on the day ahead and take the time to think on the opportunities that lie ahead, the people I will meet and coach, the fun we will have in the session (yes, it's great fun) and how lucky I am to be doing a job I love doing. Taking just that few moments helps me to be more positive about the day ahead and it will have an effect on my behaviour and the results I get.

When I first started using the *You Are The Difference* techniques back in my store in Odense, every day I would use the same technique before I opened the store in the morning. I would focus on the opportunities within the store, I would think about all the customers I would be able to talk to in order to try out my new ideas, and how much my team would get from the coaching I was to give them. Every day I did this there was always a positive result.

The next time you go to work and are about to step into your store take a moment and ask yourself how you are feeling that day.

It could be the most important question you ask that day!

THE NEG REPELLENT!

Earlier I mentioned how I gave people who like being negative the title NEG. Here is a way to deal with them the next time you feel one is beginning to pull you down the spiral.

It's your very own NEG Repellent!

It's simply a WORD and anyone can use it.

The next time you experience a NEG at work you will be able to try it out.

Picture the scene: you are on the shop floor when out of the corner of your eye you spot the NEG! The NEG is making its way towards you at speed. They have something to talk to you about and you know it's not going to be positive.

The NEG gets to you and begins to pour it out and it's <u>all</u> NEGATIVE.

When they've finished, look them in the eye and say the magic word: FANTASTIC (the NEG Repellent) then wait – the NEG will not know how to react. They will be dumb struck! You see NEG'S don't like positive words as they are not sure what to do with them.

At this point they may just turn and walk away to find another NEG to talk to.

What this will do in the store is create a bit of fun around the word FANTASTIC and people will start to get the message about the spiral.

If you feel more comfortable just thinking the word FANTASTIC then do just that, saying it to yourself WILL help keep you from being pulled down.

Always try to stay on the top of the spiral. If you do, the effect you will have on those around you will be amazing and very catching. If everyone in the team helps each other to stay at the top, think what the BUZZ in the store will be like!

But remember, wherever you are on the spiral is always <u>YOUR</u> choice!

ATTITUDE - OURS TO OWN

Earlier I talked about how the spiral was all about our attitude and how every single day we are each in control of our own. I'm sure we can all recall stories about people that have come through really tough times to make something of their lives. We tend to say that these people have a great attitude.

Attitude IS so IMPORTANT!!

Would you agree that if someone had an attitude that was **100%** positive they could achieve most things in life?

Below is a simple exercise that can help us to remember how important the word attitude really is. Listed on the left hand side is the word ATTITUDE.

Write next to each letter the number where that letter is in the alphabet.

For example, A=1, T=20 etc. then, when you have all the letters numbered simply add them up.

A –

T –

T –

I –

T –

U –

D –

E –

_____ = Total

Amazing but true!

No-one can ever choose your attitude. Where ever you are on the spiral will always be YOUR choice.

www.youarethedifference.co.uk

GREETING THE CUSTOMER

When I ask people to list the things they love to experience in service as a customer two things tend to always come top of the list: the greeting and the smile. Customers love a friendly greeting, one that makes them feel welcome in the store.

This greeting technique was the first one I developed and I haven't found anything similar in any other customer service coaching/training programme.

I was working on the Odense shop floor and had just begun looking for new ways forward in terms of customer service. Then one day, something happened.

Shortly after I had opened the store a lady came in and I greeted her in the normal way but for some reason I was aware that this time I held her eye contact for a split second longer. She greeted me back, didn't look away but held my eye contact and asked me for some hand cream. I instantly knew something different had happened, so I decided to try it again with the next customer and it worked. I greeted a man this time; he greeted me back, paused for a second and then asked me for help. It took me a little time to fully develop the technique but it soon became clear that this was an amazing technique that anyone could use to great effect.

The technique is very simple.

When we greet a customer 3 things take place:

SMILE

EYE CONTACT

VOCAL (Greeting)

In which order do you think they take place?

Most people when asked this question during a coaching session say that the eye contact comes first.

Let's step back and rewind.

Imagine I am a customer and I walk into the area where you are working in your shop. You want to greet me and you decide to use eye contact as the first form of contact with me. If I walk near you and happen to be looking the other way or straight ahead and you try to get my attention by just looking at me, imagine what that would look like!

As you can see it doesn't really work. Imagine if it were both the eye contact and the smile that were 1 and 2? It would look very strange having someone staring and grinning in silence at the customers.

So which one MUST come first?

Answer: The **GREETING**

Here is how it works:

1. *GREETING*

2. *EYE CONTACT*

3. *SMILE*

The greeting can be whatever you are comfortable with. For example, hello, good morning, or hi, are all good. What is important is that it's genuine and friendly. It must also be loud enough so the customer can hear you (sometimes there is a lot of background noise in a store).

Also important is that the greeting is not made too near the entrance to the store, if this happens the greeting technique will not work to its full potential. Always allow the customer to get fully into the store before using the greeting technique.

Why is it important that we hold eye contact with the customer when we greet them?

Because it tells the customer that:

We are friendly.

We are trustworthy.

We are aware that they have entered the store.

And most importantly, because we want to get a **RESPONSE** from the customer.

When we greet the customer she/he will respond in two possible ways.
I call these:

Eye Contact 1 and **Eye Contact 2**

Eye Contact 1:

This is the most frequent response.

STEP 1. We greet the customer (say hi, hello or good morning), make good eye contact and smile.

STEP 2. The customer makes eye contact, says hello and looks away.

What do you think this MEANS?

Usual answers are:

The customer doesn't need any help.

The customer is in a rush.

The customer is ok.

What this really means is that the customer is fine at that moment.
If at some point later that same customer needed help and you were the one that greeted them, it's most likely that you would be the person they would approach for help.

When you greet a customer and you get eye contact you create what I call an invisible bond through the eye contact. It needs to be done naturally without coming across as rehearsed. Simply say hello, make eye contact and smile then wait for the response - it will come.

Naturally, this provokes some questions, such as:

Q. *What happens if the customer is surprised when greeted?*

    A. This can happen but only in a positive way. It may after all, be the first time a sales person in a store has said hello to them in a very long time.

Q. *What if customers don't want to be greeted?*

    A. In reality customers like to be greeted when they shop. It makes them feel important and valued. Ever been in a store where you felt invisible?

Q. *How long do I have to hold the eye contact for?*

A. It's only a split second but it can feel like a little longer when you first start using the technique.

Many customers do shop alone, perhaps live alone, so being greeted by someone in a shop may well be the only contact that person has that day. If you asked that customer you greeted what they remembered most when they went shopping that day, they might well comment on the friendly greeting they received before they even begin to mention the products they looked at or bought!
The greeting in a store is a vital part of the overall customer service.

Eye Contact 2:

Eye contact 2 is a little different from 1.
Remember the elephant and the stick story where we talked about crossing an imaginary line?
With this technique you will be asked to do just that -
CROSS THAT LINE!

STEP 1 As in eye contact 1 greet the customer, make good eye contact and smile.
STEP 2 The customer makes good eye contact, says hello but this time holds eye contact and doesn't say anything.

What do you think you should do next?
The usual answers are to ask the customer:
"Can I help you?" *or* "Are you alright there?"

On most occasions the customer will reply:
"Just looking thanks!"
- leaving us feeling a little rejected.

When you greet the customer and they respond as shown in STEP 2 on the previous page simply hold eye contact and wait a split second, the customer will then usually respond with a question.

For example, "How much does that coat on display cost?" or "Where can I find your range of...."

You will simply PULL a question and that QUESTION often leads directly to a sale.

If a customer asked the cost of a coat you have on display, would you have to sell them the idea of a coat? NO! You would simply need to discover what size/colour they needed etc. You would be well on your way to making a sale. This does not mean that you are standing there staring at customers; far from it, it's only a split second.

Old habits die hard so be careful when you first start using this technique as the famous "CAN I HELP YOU?" question can just pop out naturally! This can induce a negative response. Instead, just say hello, make eye contact and smile then wait - eye contact 1 or 2 WILL happen.

The first time the eye contact 2 technique works for you let the whole team know.

This will motivate and encourage everyone to succeed with greeting the customer.

REMEMBER:
You can never fail - unless you stop. If you don't get the technique right first time don't give up, keep going. You will master it in time.

A RELAXED APPROACH

Ask anyone that works on the shop floor how they feel about approaching the customer and I am sure many would say that they dreaded it. It's that awkward moment when a sales person has to go up to a total stranger and try to engage them in conversation without looking like they are going to try and sell them something. I personally always found it hard when I had to approach a customer. So finding a technique that helped me to feel at ease when approaching was very important.

If we looked inside a store on any given day and froze the action we would see lots of customers on the shop floor all doing different things; some would be walking around browsing; some may be at the till buying goods while some others would be giving off what we call 'APPROACH' signals (they look like they need some help).

Please list below some of the things a customer could be doing that you would consider to be an approach signal:

APPROACH SIGNALS

•

•

•

•

•

Ok, so now we know what to look for.

If you would like to see some of the approach signals people have listed from previous *You Are The Difference* sessions please turn to page 94.

Now, how should we react when this happens?

Getting the approach right is vital if we are to help the customer to feel relaxed in our store. If the approach is too aggressive we run the risk of making the customer feel pounced on.

Also important to consider is what happens to the sales person's confidence when a customer reacts negatively after being approached in the wrong way. When this happens the sales person may then think twice about approaching the next customer and a sales opportunity could be lost.

Imagine that every time a customer has reacted negatively to an approach she/he would collect a yellow sticker stuck on their back with the words SPOILT written in bold black ink.

Imagine just how many yellow stickers customers could be walking around with stuck to their backs when they are out shopping!

When a customer has been spoilt over and over, store after store, day after day, customers tend to defend themselves by saying, "Just looking thanks!" when approached by a sales person. "Just looking thanks!" becomes a kind of defence mechanism in reaction to continual negative shopping experiences.

So let's now look at how we can approach the customer in a much more relaxed way, one that we can use on any customer and is how I feel WE would like to be approached when we shop.

Imagine a customer is giving off an approach signal in your store (they are for example looking through some products on a hanging rail or on a shelf). You notice they have been doing this for some time and they now look like they need some help. If you then decide to work nearby, perhaps about 10 to 12 feet away (tidying stock, cleaning etc.) would you agree that the customer will now be aware of your presence? In most cases they will.

Have you ever noticed that when you are doing a task like tidying up stock, customers often come up to you and ask for help?

If you continue to perform the task and wait a few seconds the customer may look up and ask for help or they may even come over to you to ask.

If the customer doesn't react but keeps on giving off the approach signal keep doing the task and then greet them by saying hi, good morning or hello - whatever you feel comfortable with. If the customer greets you back but then looks away and continues looking through the rack they are simply telling you that they are fine at that point in time (eye contact 1). Just stay close as they may need help at a later stage, if they do it will be you they will ask.

There are of course other things you could say to the customer if they don't react to you working nearby them, (you may also have already greeted them in store) for example, "What size do you need?" or "Those are all new colours!" or "That's a really nice style!"

Just don't ask the customer "Need any help?" or "Are you allright there?" as that almost always provokes the negative reaction of, "Just looking thanks!" and you would have just SPOILT another customer!

Put yourself in the shoes of the customer; what would you prefer?

Option 1
That the sales person comes straight up to you and asks "Need any help?" or "Are you allright there?"
Or:
Option 2
That the sales person works close by giving you the opportunity to approach them, or that they simply greet you or make a comment after giving you some time and space?

I'm sure you would choose Option 2.

So there it is. That is the approach technique. Simple and easy to use and it's how I'm sure we all would like to be approached as a customer.

People buy people first, the product second!

PERFECT PARTNERS

Perfect Partners is not a new dating agency but a simple way to introduce a product that complements the product or service the customer is buying.

Link selling as it's called, can sound and feel a little pushy and some sales people do find the technique difficult to perform. I set out to find a more relaxed way to introduce complementary products and it became Perfect Partners. The technique cannot in any way be termed pushy. It comes naturally as part of finalising the sale.

The easy way to BRING two products together.

At the end of the sale when the customer has decided to purchase a shirt for example you would simply say, "By the way have you seen our range of ties, there are some that would really go well with the shirt?"

(Keep it relaxed and just mention the complementary product - don't at this stage go into too much detail)

No customer to my knowledge has ever exclaimed:
"Right that's it; I'm not having the shirt now as you pointed out those ties!"
However what can happen is as follows:

1. The customer looks at the ties and chooses one that complements the shirt. (Additional sale)

2. The customer says, "No thanks" and buys the shirt.
(However she/he is now aware that you have ties)

Many customers DO decide to buy the product or service that complements their purchase because the original product becomes MORE when it's teamed up with its Perfect Partner! If the customer decides not to take up your offer then at least she/he now knows about the complementary product and they may purchase it at some later date.
The key to success is to introduce the Perfect Partner at the END of the sale once the customer has decided to buy the first product.

REMEMBER:
It's always a no until you ask the question so just ask!

CLOSING THE SALE

Closing a sale at the end of a conversation with a customer can sometimes be a little awkward.

Some sales people just continue talking to the customer hoping they will be interrupted by the comment, "Ok I will take it," while other sales people just stop talking altogether and wait for the customer to close it for them!

The following closing technique is simple, effective and one that always works!

When you are ready to close the sale just ask this simple question...

Is there anything else you NEED today?

The customer will then do one of two things.

They will either say: "No that's everything I need today," (you have now closed the sale) or, they will think for a moment and say, "Actually do you have such and such a product?" but either way you have still closed the sale.

The great thing about this technique is you can ask the customer the question more than once. Let's say the customer responds with, "Yes, I need a belt for these trousers I have just bought." After you help to find the belt, you can then ask the question again, "Is there any thing else you need?" Why should we decide when the customer is finished shopping?

The magic word here is NEED. When I started working on this technique, I tried many different questions such as, "Is there anything else I can help you with?" or, "Is there anything else I can show you?" but none of these worked as well as the NEED question. The word NEED triggers the memory and makes the customer think, "Do I need anything else today?"

How many times have you come home from shopping, put down all the bags then thought, "OH NO! I forgot to get it!" as you realise you do not have the thing you actually went out shopping for? If someone had asked you in the store at the end of the sale, "Is there anything else you need today?" you probably would have remembered the thing you have now come home without!

When you want to close the sale ask the question,

"IS THERE ANYTHING ELSE YOU NEED TODAY?"

Then wait for the customer to answer. If there is a pause, try not to break the silence - the customer is just thinking. If you do break it with a comment there is a real chance the customer will say, "No thanks," perhaps losing you an extra sale.

By giving the customer time to think you allow them the opportunity to remember those things they actually need to get that day and many of those things may well be in your store.

Use this truly powerful question at the end of every sale and experience the positive results you will achieve with it.

PRODUCT IN THE HAND

Now we come to one of the most powerful and exciting techniques within *You Are The Difference*, the product in the hand.

This skill, once mastered will give you the edge when it comes to interacting with the customer. All it takes is practice and a little confidence.

The history behind the technique is an interesting one and one I feel worth sharing.

It all came about quite by accident, one day while working on the Odense shop floor with a customer at the make-up stand. At that time I had a system where I would write ideas and experiences I had with customers in a small book. I would scribble down notes after I had tried something new and then at the end of the day I would sit down and go through all the notes one by one to try and see if there was anything that was worth developing further.

Usually there were lots of things I couldn't use. Sometimes, I would strike gold and with this technique I knew I had found something special.

Below is a copy of what I had written that day.

> Customer at make-up stand put back the mascara tester we were talking about. I then asked her to confirm the colour she used and placed the actual product in her hand and said "there it is there" the customer said "thank you" and bought it!

I asked myself why had that worked?

The next day, I decided to try out the technique again so I placed different products in customers' hands during the sale process. To my amazement at the end of the conversation many customers bought the product.

So here is the technique:

When you are with the customer and you are talking about a product they are interested in and it's one that can easily be handled, simply place the product in the customer's hand and make a comment. It could be, "There it is there, feel the quality of the material, see how small and light it is.

You can also at this time mention instructions or special information about the product that you feel could be of interest to the customer.

Be sure to place the product in their hand so they can see the information clearly. When you do this, point to the information or characteristics of the product. Then watch what the customer does.

The customer will look down at the product and take in the information they feel is important to them. This is always a good point to name some of the benefits or special characteristics the product has but try to keep this short and simple.

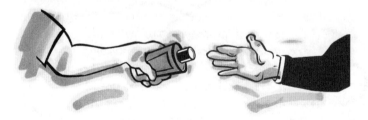

After you have given the customer all the information they need about the product and they keep on holding it, ask them the question, "Is there anything else you need today?"

If the customer pauses and then replies, "No" and they continue to hold on to the product then it's almost certain they are going to buy it!

If they say, "Yes" then there is potentially another sale.

This technique requires confidence and timing: when you place the product in the customer's hand you must do it without hesitation; it must look natural and the timing must be right, not too early or too late in the sale. When you feel you have established some rapport with the customer that's usually the best time to do it.

Why does it work so well?

I think it comes down to ownership; when we hold a product in our hand for some time, it almost becomes ours through the touch and feel.

I have had some memorable experiences with this technique. One that sticks out in my mind was in a large store in Oxford Street, London. I was demonstrating a warming mask cream when a group of women entered the store.

As I started to explain the benefits of the mask to one of the women from the group I placed the product (mask) in her hand and as she was looking at it, I also placed the mask in the hands of all the other women that were in the group.

At the end of the demonstration I used the technique to close the sale and the woman I originally placed the product with bought the mask, but to my amazement so did many of the other women from the group who were continuing to hold onto the mask I had placed in their hands! Placing the product in the customer's hand does take a little time to perfect but once mastered you will have raised your customer serivce skills to a whole new level.

Customers do US a favour by coming to see us. We are not doing them a favour by serving them.

THE FITTING ROOM

The Fitting Room- that special place in a store where you can meet the customer, build rapport, introduce Perfect Partners and make a lasting impression through the service you give.

THE INITIAL CONTACT:
Greet the customer as she/he approaches you with products to try on.

ESTABLISHING THE CUSTOMER'S NEEDS:
Does the customer have the correct products?
Colour? Size? Range?

BUILDING RAPPORT:
You may be with the customer for a period of time in the fitting room so it's important you establish a good rapport with them.

MAKING SUGGESTIONS:
When the customer is in the fitting room encourage them to come out and show you how the product looks on them. Suggestions and compliments can also be made at this time.

PERFECT PARTNERS:
Here is the ideal opportunity to suggest to the customer a product that would compliment the one they are trying on. A good idea can be to have some Perfect Partners ready to hand.

THE CLOSE:
After the customer has finished trying on the product and you want to close the sale ask the question,
"Is there anything else you need today?"

Great service in the fitting room begins and ends with YOU.

Last impressions really do count.

THE FAB FIVE: AT THE TILL

Let's imagine you are out shopping and you receive really great service on the shop floor but when you go to the till the service you experience there is very bad.
What do you remember from this experience?
Is it the service on the shop floor? Or, is it the service at the till? In almost all cases people remember the LAST thing they experience. Every single product that is sold in most stores goes through the till. The service the customer receives at the till is VITAL as it's the last experience in the store and it does create an all-important lasting impression.

Here are 5 simple steps that you can do at the till that will create a great last impression:

Greet
Thank for waiting
Positive comment
Pack well
Thank you: Goodbye

THE FAB FIVE

1. **GREET**: Say hello to the customer, make eye contact and smile.

2. **THANK FOR WAITING**: If the customer has had to wait just say, "Thanks for waiting," and smile. We all know what it's like to be in a long queue getting more and more frustrated as time goes by, if this had happened to us and the person at the till had said, "Thanks for waiting," we are more likely to reply, "That's ok." Saying this to the customers does help diffuse the situation and always works better than saying, "Sorry to keep you waiting" which is usually perceived as a negative apology.

3. **POSITIVE COMMENT**: Make a positive comment about the product the customer is purchasing. It doesn't have to be a long conversation; a simple, "That's nice," or "I like that colour," is fine. Giving the customer a positive comment reinforces the good feeling they have about their purchase.

4. **PACK WELL**: Ever gone to the till with your new product and you are thinking to yourself how much you are going to enjoy using or wearing it, and then at the till the sales person throws it into a bag with no care? How does that make you feel? How we pack the product is very important because when a customer takes a product to the till in her/his mind they now own it so it needs to be treated with the care it deserves.

5. **THANK AND SAY GOODBYE**: This is the final part of the Fab Five and the one that brings it all together at the till. If the customer receives great service at the till up to this point but the sales person forgets to say thank you and good bye or rushes to get to the next customer then the last impression is spoilt. Every single customer deserves a "Thank you" and a "Goodbye" when they leave the store.

THE MAGNIFICENT SEVEN: RECAP

1. *THE SPIRAL*
It's always going to be your choice where you are on the spiral: Focus on the positives and the opportunities around you then see how quickly this positive effect rubs off on the people you work with and on the customer.

2. *THE GREETING*
By using the greeting technique you will instantly create an invisible bond with the customer through the eye contact. The response you get from the customer after you greet them will tell you if they are OK or if they want to ask you a question. (Eye contact 1 and 2)

3. *THE APPROACH*
This can be the one thing sales people dread. This approach technique will help you to approach the customer in a simple and relaxed way putting you and the customer at ease.

4. *PERFECT PARTNERS*
The easy way to introduce a product that compliments the one the customer is buying. This technique quickly becomes a natural part of every sale. No pressure - it's perfect!

5. *CLOSING THE SALE*
A simple question at the end of every sale, "Is there anything else you need today?" If the customer replies with a yes or a no you have either closed the sale or discovered something else the customer needs.

6. *PRODUCT IN THE HAND*
The touch and feel of a product can be magical. Once mastered, this exciting technique will have raised your shop floor skills to a whole new level.

7. *THE FAB FIVE*
Five simple things that you can do at the till when serving the customer that will create that great last impression before they leave the store.

If you think you can or you think you can't you are right.

CATCH A BUTTERFLY

The skills and techniques you have now discovered all DO work, but there is one condition attached to them: they only work if YOU do!

You may find that some techniques work for you first time and other may take you a little longer to master. The important thing is you should not give up. You can master them all. When it comes to developing any new kind of skill it's a bit like forming a new habit and that can take around a month to really take hold.

Try not to put yourself under too much pressure to begin with. Don't expect to get it all perfect first time. If you are determined to succeed just keep on trying and it will all fall into place in time.

GET EXCITED!

That fantastic feeling you will experience when a new technique works for you the very first time is special and one you will instantly recognise.

When we try new things we need to be ready to step outside our comfort zone and when we do this we can get that butterfly feeling inside. It's healthy to have those butterflies; that's EXCITEMENT working for you.

If you have never felt the butterflies when you are on the shop floor then you may not be stepping outside your comfort zone. Take action and make it happen using these skills and techniques. Don't think about it, just do it, get EXCITED!

BABY STEPS

When it comes to learning anything new it's important to take just one step at a time and not put yourself under too much pressure. The same applies to learning the skills and techniques in this book. Take one skill/technique and master it before moving onto the next. Doing this will help build your confidence.

It is important that every day you give yourself some honest feedback. Look at what happened when you used the skill/ technique, ask yourself what went well and what you would do differently to improve it next time. Then give yourself some praise; after all you have earned it!

REACH FOR YOUR BEST

When you walk on to the shop floor you take with you all that you are. Although you may have checked yourself in the mirror beforehand – hair, make-up, clothes, and shoes –you will only have seen the external part of you. Personal presentation is important but inner style - that comes from confidence.

If you are self-confident it shows in your body language, in your face and in the words you use. Working with customers does require a certain amount of confidence so it's important that you focus on the things you do well, so that you feel a positive self belief.

When you step on to the shop floor every day, take all of you with you. Think about your strengths, what you are good at and all you have achieved so far.

Reach for your best and make each day count.

YOUR STRENGTHS

What do you believe are your strengths? Think long and hard about your positive qualities. Don't hold back on this - go on be nice to yourself. Imagine that someone else is looking at you; what are the strengths they can see? Now list them below starting each one with: I am...

"I am..."

"I am..."

"I am..."

"I am..."

"I am..."

"I am..."

"I am..."

"I am..."

"I am..."

"I am..."

And this is just the start! If you were given more lines to complete, in no time you would be able to fill them all with even more strengths. Focusing on your list of strengths from time to time will help you to build your positive self belief and inner confidence. Helping you to reach for your best.

THE ROLE OF THE MANAGER In *You Are The Difference*

The key in keeping the *You Are The Difference* coaching programme alive on the shop floor is down to the commitment and the action taken by the store manager - FACT!

In order for the new skills and techniques to become embedded into the store's daily routine the manager must lead from the front by regularly coaching her/his sales team and by displaying that they themselves use the *You Are The Difference* skills and techniques on the shop floor with the customer. When a manager does all of these things they will keep the 'buzz' from the initial coaching session alive and encourage the sales team to keep on using the new skills. The *You Are The Difference* programme will then become part of the service culture in the store.

In the real world of course all managers have pressures on their time during the day. These pressures could be looked at as a type of barrier that could get in the way, stopping a manager from achieving any of the above i.e. serving customers (leading from the front) and in coaching his/her sales team. On the next page is a simple exercise that can help a manager along the path to finding the key to achieving the above.

If you as a manager want to know who is most responsible for where the sales team focus on the shop floor is: take a look in the mirror.

THE BARRIERS

1. List below all the tasks and activities that could prevent you, as a manager, from serving customers and coaching your sales team on the shop floor.

2. Place a percentage (%) next to each task/activity on your list in terms of the time each day spent on it. (Approximately)

....

....

....

....

....

....

....

....

....

Your list should now represent the approximate percentage of time your barriers take up on any given day.

The things that matter most must never be at the mercy of those which matter least.

Johanne Goethe

THE CIRCLE OF CONTROL

If you agree that the customer is the number one priority, i.e. the thing that matters most, then where is the customer in all of this?

At this point some managers may be thinking, "All the barriers I have listed are taking up all of my time! I want to drive the *You Are The Difference* programme in my store and make it work but how can I find the time to coach my sales team and serve customers?"

Help is at now at hand....

Introducing: The Circle of Control by Steven Covey

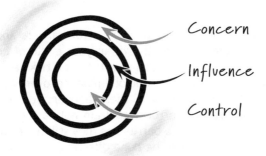

Concern

Influence

Control

In life we all have concerns, e.g. our health, our children, our family, problems at work etc. Some of these we have control and influence over and others we don't. As you can see above we have a series of circles. In the outer circle sits the things we are concerned about but cannot influence or control. Moving inwards we have the circle of influence, some of our concerns will sit here within this circle, as we may be able to influence them. Then finally moving into the centre we have the circle of control; in here are all the concerns we have total control over.

Let's look at an example: In the circle of concern you may be really concerned that it's going to rain at the weekend but there is obviously nothing you can do about the weather. In the circle of influence you may be concerned that your sales team are not giving the level of customer service you would like to see in your store. You as a manager do have some influence over this as you manage your team on a daily basis. Then finally in the circle of control you may have a concern that you will use the new *You Are The Difference* skills and techniques; here you obviously have total control.

Proactive people go to work on their concerns within their circles of influence and control and by doing so their influence and control increases. Reactive people on the other hand spend time worrying about concerns they have no influence or control over and as a result their circle of influence and control get smaller.

Now have another look at your list of barriers and decide which of them are actually within your circle of control or influence? As you go through your list put a tick next to those you feel you have any control/influence over. As you will discover there are many of these barriers you do actually have influence or control over. I am not saying you should just forget about these barriers as they still need to be done but perhaps they could be done differently or at a different time? Could some of them be delegated?

If you are truly committed to the *You Are The Difference* programme then taking influence or control over some or all of these barriers is the key to its success. As manager you must be able to free up some of your time during the day to use The Five Stages of Coaching (on page 88) with your sales team and lead from the front on the shop floor.

If as a manager you lead then the team will follow.

COACHING

Coaching is a tool that will enable you to spend more time with your sales team on the shop floor. But what is coaching?

What is it that comes to mind when you read the word 'coaching'?
Here are some examples people attending *The Role of the Manager* in *You Are The Difference* sessions have given:

- *Encouragement*
- *Being Supportive*
- *Training*
- *Developing Potential*
- *Motivation*
- *Improving Performance*

If these listed above are some of the things coaching represents then what are the QUALITIES of a good coach?
Take a moment and think back to a time when someone coached you, for example: at school, in sport, at work. When you have recalled this experience think about the qualities that coach/teacher in question had; what was it they possessed that made them such a good coach?

Here are some examples people have given:

- *Good Listener*
- *Supportive*
- *Patient*
- *Good Observer*
- *Attentive*
- *Interested*

We have now looked at WHAT coaching is and the QUALITIES a good coach should have but just how SHOULD we coach?
Here are the *You Are The Difference* Five Stages of Coaching.

THE FIVE STAGES OF COACHING

1. OBSERVE
Observe a sales person on the shop floor with a customer throughout a sale.

2. ASK HOW IT WENT
Once the sale is over ask the sales person to talk through the sale with you.

3. ASK HOW IT COULD BE DONE DIFFERENTLY
After the sales person has gone through the sale ask what they would do differently next time?

This gives the sales person the opportunity to think about how they would improve the sale. It's like a form of self-coaching. If the sales person suggests something they could do to improve the sale they are more likely to remember it next time, as they were the one who came up with the suggestion.

4. MAKE SUGGESTIONS
If you still feel there is something the sales person could do to improve the sale then it's at this point the suggestion should be made.

5. PRAISE
At the end of the conversation give the sales person praise and encouragement; doing this will motivate them to keep working with the new skills and techniques and to improve on the sale.

By regularly using the Five Stages of Coaching on the shop floor a manager will be able to keep the whole team focussed on the You Are The Difference skills and techniques cementing the coaching programme long term.

THE B-ALERT

A proven checkpoint system for creating positive results with the *You Are The Difference* customer service coaching programme everyday.

B-
BLUEPRINT
The *You Are The Difference* programme aims and goals for your store that week.

A-
ACTION
Daily focus on one *You Are The Difference* skill and the action plan that will see it through.

L-
LEARNING
The Five Stages of coaching

E-
ENERGIZE
Focus on positive language and the spiral.

R-
REVIEW
Take time to reflect on the day. Review goals, develop new ideas.

T-
THANK
Catch the sales team doing something well and praise them.

By using the B-ALERT Checkpoint System every day a manager will have a helpful reminder of those activities that are key to keeping You Are The Difference Customer Service Programme alive on the shop floor.

You can track your progress by recording your results on the B-ALERT found within the special coaching pack or by setting up your own simple recording chart, as in the example below. Circle any area that you miss (columns with no ticks or circles are days not worked).

MON	TUES	WED	THUR	FRI	SAT	SUN
✔B	B	✔B	✔B	✔B	✔B	B
✔A	A	✔A	✔A	✔A	✔A	A
✔L	L	(L)	✔L	✔L	✔L	L
(E)	E	✔E	✔E	(E)	✔E	E
✔R	R	✔R	✔R	✔R	✔R	R
✔T	T	✔T	✔T	✔T	✔T	T

At the end of each day ask yourself if you focused on all six parts of the B-ALERT System. Be honest with your evaluation. You will notice patterns developing each week that will highlight what you are doing well and what you need to focus more on.Use a red pen to circle the letters you feel there is room for improvement. For example if plan to carry out shop floor coaching every day and you notice the letter L has 3 red circles drawn around it in the week,you need to make some changes! As always ease into this new habit. Don't be too hard on yourself at the start.The more you practice, the better results you will have.

MY COMMITMENT AS A MANAGER

Here is your opportunity as a manager to make your commitment to the *You Are The Difference* programme.

I ....

Commit myself to finding the time I need to coach my sales team on the shop floor and to lead from the front by using the *You Are The Difference* skills and techniques when serving customers.

Signature......................................

Date...

Desire is the key to motivation, but it's determination and commitment in persuit of your goal – a commitment to excellence – that will enable you to attain the success you seek.

Mario Andretti

NOTHING HAPPENS UNTIL YOU TAKE ACTION

The words within these pages are just that - WORDS. It is you who will bring them to life when you use the skills and techniques described in the book.

The choice is yours. You can put this book down and continue as before or you can choose to change and use the skills and techniques to make a difference to you and your store.

If you have read this far then you are open to change and the challenge. Take ACTION now and start to make it happen. Take that first step!

To demonstrate the power of taking action in my sessions, I hold up a £10 note and ask, "Who can have this £10 pound note?" Usually most people in the audience will raise their hands. Some will wave their hands vigorously back and forth; some will even shout "I can have it" or "Give it to me." But then I just stand there asking, "Who can have it?" until the penny drops. Eventually, someone jumps from her/his seat and takes the note from my hand.

After the person sits down - now £10 richer for her/his efforts -I ask the audience, "What was it this person did that no one else in the room did?" They took action.

If your ship doesn't come in, swim out to meet it.

Jonathan Winters

Here are some of the TOP Loves and Loathes suggested during *You Are The Difference* Sessions.

LOVE

✔ Being greeted with a smile

✔ Interest being shown in me as a customer

✔ A relaxed approach by the sales staff

✔ Good manners on the shop floor and at the till

✔ Staff willing to go the 'extra mile' for me

LOATHE !@^*^@*

✗ Being ignored as I enter the store and on the shop floor

✗ Staff giving off negative body language

✗ Being pounced on by sales staff

✗ Poor manners on the sales floor and at the till

✗ Being made to feel inferior

Here are some of the TOP approach signals suggested by people that have attended the *You Are The Difference* Session.

- The customer is standing looking at a range of products or a display for a long period of time

- The customer is wandering around the store looking a little lost

- The customer is trying to attract the attention of a sales person

- The customer has been searching through a range of products for a long period of time

- The customer is holding up two products comparing them against each other

- The customer is standing looking at a shopping list

- The customer has been reading the information on the product for a long period of time

- The customer has their arms full of product and continues to shop

My goal was to write a book that incorporated the **You Are The Difference** customer service principles that I have been coaching through my work for the past 10 years. This is the book you are reading.

In order to achieve this goal I sought the help and support of many people and had it not been for their encouragement this book would never have been completed. There have been many times I have sat down to write and found myself nowhere near the top of my spiral and in no mood to be creative, but I have remembered the principles of the spiral and focused on my attitude and the opportunities I had in being able to share the principles of **You Are The Difference**. I have also needed to remind myself on many occasions why writing this book is so important to me. There are many reasons, including a desire to see the **You Are The Difference** message spread beyond the people I am fortunate enough to coach.

I admit I also want the book to raise my profile, which in my business is important. I also want to leave a legacy to my children. This is a little of my story and the journey I took to achieving my goal. What will your story be?

How will you use the **You Are The Difference** principles to help you achieve your goals?

I wish you success on your journey, please let me know how **You Are The Difference** helps.

Alf Dunbar

It is the big choices we make that set our direction. It is the smallest choices we make that get us to the destination.

If you want to know more about *You Are The Difference* then visit www.youarethedifference.co.uk where you can share your thoughts on how *You Are The Difference* has helped you and learn how it has helped others.

You can also contact Alf at: alf@youarethedifference.co.uk

Bring Alf to your company or organisation:

You can bring Alf into your company or organisation to deliver the principles of this book.
For more details visit **www.youarethedifference.co.uk**

If you prefer you can contact us at our office.
You Are The Difference
Ashwood House
47E Kingsgate
Aberdeen
AB15 4EL
Scotland
Tel: + 44 (0) 7720 295296

Copies of this book, the *You Are The Difference* coaching DVD where Alf presents the main skills and techniques from the customer service programme and a coaching disc with Powerpoint slides/script can be ordered at:
sales@youarethedifference.co.uk

The *You Are The Difference* Coaching DVD carries subtitles in:

Danish
French
German
Russian
Spanish

You Are The Difference in schools and hospitals

Alf is keen to hear from anyone who is interested in developing and using the *You Are The Difference* motivational and attitudinal principles inside schools and hospitals. If that's you, then please contact us.
We look forward to hearing from you.

Editor: joyce@arribamarketing.co.uk
Photo: www.firstphotographics.co.uk
Reprographics: www.repro-overflow.com
Website: www.orangespongemonkey.com
DVD production: www.eastside-productions.co.uk
Illustrations redrawn: lesclarkart@btopenworld.com

NOTES

ISBN 141209413-5